Baseball's Best
Barbs,
Banter,
and
Bluster

Dick Crouser

TRIUMPH
B O O K S
CHICAGO

Library of Congress Cataloging-in-Publication Data

Crouser, Dick.
    Baseball's best barbs, banter, and bluster / Dick Crouser.
        p. cm.
    ISBN 1-57243-644-1
        1. Baseball—United States—Humor. 2. Baseball players—United States—Anecdotes. I. Title.

GV873.C76 2004
796.357—dc22

2004041249

This book is available in quantity at special discounts for your group or organization. For further information, contact:
    Triumph Books
    601 South LaSalle Street
    Suite 500
    Chicago, Illinois 60605
    (312) 939-3330
    Fax (312) 663-3557

Printed in U.S.A.
ISBN 1-57243-644-1
Design by Patricia Frey
Illustrations by Mark Anderson

CONTENTS

INTRODUCTION

When a fella can combine
two of his favorite things
and actually get paid for it,
well, it just doesn't get any
better than that. I'm kicked
back in a lounge chair,
surrounded by books,
newspapers, and magazines,
in search of the snappiest
punch lines, the funniest
put-downs, and the greatest
comeback lines from the
wonderful world of baseball.

The missus, passing through and noticing that I

seem to be enjoying myself rather excessively,

interrupts: "What are you doing and why aren't you

mowing the lawn?" "Sorry, dear," I reply solemnly, "I'm working."

Humor and baseball. A delightful pair. A natural pair. Because with all its frustrations, tensions, absurdities, and cruel twists of fate, baseball provides a rich and fertile field for humor.

There's no sport to match it for fun and games. For fun and gamesmanship.

Take Dizzy Dean, a baseball great both on the mound and on the mic. It is a huge understatement to say that he knew how to pitch. But anyone who knew him will vouch for the man's ability to "talk a good game," too.

In 1934 Diz and his brother Paul won 49 games between them (30 and 19, respectively) and led the St. Louis Cardinals to the N.L. pennant. In a late-season doubleheader Dizzy threw a three-hitter in the opener, and Paul followed with a no-hitter.

Why was Dizzy unhappy?

"If I'da knowd Paul was gonna get him a no-hitter," said Diz, "I'da got one too."

Yes, the snappy comeback line, the wisecrack, is something of an American art form. It thrives across the whole spectrum of American sports and is at its absolute best in the world of professional baseball.

Let me give you some examples—more than three hundred of them, to be exact.

Baseball's Best
Barbs,
Banter,
and
Bluster

Chapter 1

THE PLAYERS, PART I

YOU JUST CAN'T COUNT ON PETE

Who is the king of the witty baseball retort? Well, no matter how you feel about Pete Rose, you have to admit that he ranks right up there in the sharp-tongue department. In fact, let the record show that only once in his 24-year career was he caught speechless.

Day 1: Left fielder Alex Johnson and Rose, playing center, converged on a fly ball. As the ball popped out of Johnson's glove, Rose grabbed it for the out (possibly the only 7-8 putout in the history of baseball).

Day 2: A line drive was hit right at Johnson and he dropped it. Without missing a beat he turned over toward Rose and yelled, "Where *were* you?!"

3

Pitcher Sal Maglie was called "the Barber" because of his readiness to administer a close shave to any batter digging in on him. As any National League hitter from the fifties can attest, the nickname was well earned. Part of Maglie's knockdown procedure was to throw not one but two brushbacks at a hitter. "The second one," he explained, "lets him know you meant the first one."

For all the great numbers outfielder Gary Sheffield has put up, his personality still gets him a few detractors. The *San Francisco Chronicle*'s Tom Fitzgerald is one of them: "Sheffield is such a fine player that three cities are named after him," he

4

wrote. "Gary, Indiana; Sheffield, England; and Marblehead, Massachusetts."

Through the 2000 season, outfielder Luis Polonia's lifetime batting average was just a hair under .300, but according to former teammate Dennis Lamp, his fielding was a bit shaky. "If you hit Polonia a hundred fly balls," he said, "you could make a movie out of it and call it *Catch 22.*"

Gates Brown's path to a 13-year career in the big leagues was a bit unorthodox. The Tigers signed him right out of prison in the early sixties. Invited back to his old high school for a success-story speech, Brown was asked by the principal what he had taken at Crestline High. "Overcoats, mainly," said Gates.

With the DH in force, pitcher Jimmy Key wound up his 15-year American League career in 1998 with just two official at-bats. That might explain his faux pas in a spring-training game while with the Blue Jays. Called upon to pinch hit when no one else was available, he lined a shot into right field but was thrown out at first. "They told me to hit," he said. "Nobody said anything about running."

> Ex–Atlanta Braves pitcher Tom Glavine signed with the Mets for the 2003 season and, in his *first* outing, was facing only his second hitter when the notorious New York boo-birds turned on him. An onlooker called it the shortest honeymoon in history not involving someone named Zsa Zsa.

The *San Francisco Chronicle*'s Scott Ostler reported on some early 2003 progress in the negotiations between Pete Rose and commissioner Bud Selig to lift Rose's ban from baseball. Ostler reported that Pete's latest counteroffer was that he would agree to be reinstated if Selig would admit that he once sold used cars.

Barry Bonds has received his six MVP Awards on the basis of his performance, not his personality. He once discussed a recent slump while seated at his locker. "It was a terrible experience," he said. "It was awful, I felt so depressed." Then, turning to a teammate at the next locker, he said, "You must feel like that *all* the time."

First baseman Zeke Bonura, who was traded from Jimmy Dykes' White Sox to the Washington Senators in 1938, was considered the slowest runner in the history of baseball. He was perhaps not the most quick-witted, either. The first time the teams played each other after the trade, Bonura tried to steal home and was thrown out by 30 feet. Why did he even try? "I saw Dykes give the steal sign," said Bonura, "and I forgot I didn't play for him anymore."

Sweet-swinging Billy Williams had Pittsburgh hurler Steve Blass for breakfast.

Outfielder Billy Williams gave lots of pitchers plenty of trouble during his 18-year career, but the Pirates' Steve Blass felt *constantly* picked on. Blass once pitched the first game of a Cubs holiday doubleheader that started at 10:30 A.M. Remarking on the game, he said, "I gave up three hits to Billy Williams and it wasn't even noon yet!"

Pitcher John Rocker's outspoken opinions have made him less than popular with minorities. When he was traded to the Cleveland Indians in 2001, a group of Native Americans expressed their displeasure. Rocker's reaction: "Tell them to go back where they came from."

8

Nick Etten played first base for the Yankees during the WWII years. He was a respectable hitter, but he never really sparkled in the field. Once, as he dove for a ball, his glove came off but the ball stuck in the webbing. Sportswriter Joe Trimble said, "Nick Etten's glove fields better with Nick Etten out of it."

It's all relative, according to sportswriter Scott Ostler. In 2001, when Randy Johnson blew Todd Helton away on three pitches clocked at 100, 100, and 99 mph, Ostler wrote, "The cunning lefty sets up Helton with fastballs and then gets him with a change-up."

Back when few big-league players had a college education, catcher Moe Berg was a notable exception. He had degrees from both Princeton and

Columbia Law School—and an anemic .243 lifetime batting average. "He could speak eight languages," said teammate Ted Lyons, "but he couldn't hit in any of them."

Rex Barney came up to the Dodgers in 1943 with a blazing fastball and unlimited potential. He retired in 1950 without ever learning to control his impressive heater. Sportswriter Bob Cooke delivered the postmortem: "Rex Barney would have been the league's best pitcher if the plate were high and outside."

Chapter 2

THE HALL OF
FAMERS, PART I

LEO'S
MOM

Leo Durocher did not get into the Baseball Hall of Fame in recognition of his .247 batting average over 17 years in the majors.

Officially, he was voted in by the Veterans Committee—as a manager.

But you and I know that he really got in because of his sharp tongue and fierce competitive nature. How fierce? Let's hear it from the scrappy old shortstop himself.

"If my mother is rounding second, I'd trip her. I'd help her up, brush her off, and tell her I'm sorry. But Mother doesn't make it to third base."

That's Leo the Lip. Shall we move on to the wit and wisdom of some of his Hall of Fame playmates?

Ted Williams didn't seem to have any weaknesses at the plate, and he absolutely *feasted* on pitches down around the knees. So when Cleveland manager Lou Boudreau called reliever Red Embree in from the bullpen to pitch to Williams and Embree asked, "Can I pitch him low?" Boudreau said, "You can if you want to, but as soon as you release the ball you'd better run and hide."

Star Yankees pitcher Lefty Gomez lived in mortal fear of burly Red Sox slugger Jimmy Foxx. Once, in 1938, with Foxx digging in in a crucial situation, Gomez shook off four straight signals from catcher Bill Dickey. Finally, Dickey went to the mound and said, "OK, wise guy, what *do* you want to throw?" "What's your hurry?" said Gomez. "Maybe he'll get a phone call or something."

Maurice "Mickey" McDermott had an up-and-down career, pitching for six different American League teams as well as the National League's

Cardinals. His one year with the Yankees, 1956, was in the "down" column and, once, stumbling into the team's hotel lobby at 4:00 A.M. and running smack into manager Casey Stengel, he figured it was all over. "Are you drunk again, Maurice?" asked Casey. "Yes, I am," said McDermott. "So am I," said Stengel. "Good night, Maurice."

Willie Mays' most memorable moment was his incredible catch of Vic Wertz's 460-foot blast in the 1954 World Series. The pitcher, Don Liddle, had come in just to face Wertz and threw one pitch. *One pitch*. And he was immediately replaced after the catch that resulted. As Liddle entered the dugout he said, "Well, I got *my* guy."

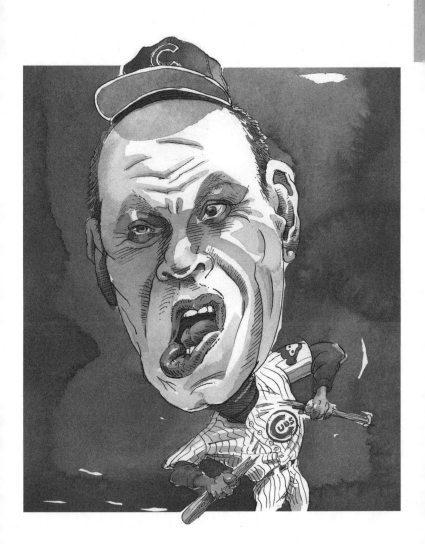

> Leo "the Lip" Durocher had a Hall-of-Fame mouth, though his bat was considerably quieter.

When Hall of Famer Stan Musial took his lifetime .331 batting average to the plate, National League pitchers trembled. But the Dodgers' Preacher Roe had his own system for dealing with Stan the Man. "I usually walk him on four pitches," said Roe, "and then try to pick him off first."

Joe DiMaggio was named to the American League All-Star Team every year he played for the Yankees—13 times altogether. He also posted an astounding .579 lifetime slugging average. And that was fine with manager Joe McCarthy. Asked if DiMaggio knew how to bunt, McCarthy said, "I will never find out."

Hall of Fame shortstop Rabbit Maranville was a scrapper, on and off the field. Bill Veeck recalled Maranville stumbling out of a hotel bar and insulting a cab driver, who then beat him up. Same result with the second cabbie in line. Same with the third. What was he doing? "Trying to find one I can whip," he explained.

The day that Lou Gehrig hit four dingers in one game, he pulled the first three into the right-field stands off George Earnshaw of the Philadelphia Athletics. As Gehrig came up for the fourth time, manager Connie Mack brought in Roy Mahaffey to pitch and suggested that Earnshaw watch how the reliever handled Gehrig. When the

Yankee slugger hit Mahaffey's first pitch into the *left*-field stands, Earnshaw said, "I see. He made him change directions."

Eppa Rixey broke in with the Phillies in 1912 and pitched in the National League for 21 years, but he never mastered his violent temper. A die-hard Southerner, he especially hated the Yankee Civil War song "Marching Through Georgia." Once, hearing it whistled in the opponents' dugout, he wheeled and fired the ball at the whistler. "It ain't that the song makes me mad," he explained. "It makes me mad that they *think* it makes me mad."

If things ever got dull in spring training, the sportswriters covering the Yankees headed right for Yogi Berra's locker. Once, when asked by a scribe what his hat size was, Yogi replied, "I don't know. I'm not in shape yet."

In 1930, Cubs manager Joe McCarthy put on a little demonstration to try to reform his hard-drinking, heavy-hitting outfielder, Hack Wilson. He dropped a worm into a glass of water and the worm swam around. He dropped the same worm into a glass of gin and the worm died. What did Hack learn from that? "If you drink gin," said Wilson, "you won't get worms."

Over a 20-year career, outfielder Paul Waner sported a .333 lifetime batting average and led the National League in hitting three times. According to some teammates, he also led the league in boozing. When Waner was with the Braves in 1942, manager Casey Stengel was especially impressed with Paul's grace on the base paths because, according to Casey, "He could slide without breaking the bottle in his back pocket."

Hard-nosed pitcher Early Wynn was offended when Washington's weak-hitting Jose Valdivielso lined one off his chin, resulting in 16 stitches. For the rest of his career, Valdivielso never batted against Wynn without getting hit or knocked down. "The mound is my office," said Wynn, "and I don't like it messed up with blood."

Reggie Jackson didn't accept the huge offer he got to play in Japan in 1988, but he thought about it. "They say it gets lonely there," he said. "But for that kind of money I could buy some friends and take them with me."

When Hank Aaron hit home run number 715 to break Babe Ruth's record, Dodgers left-hander Al Downing was the victim. Years later Downing was asked how that historic moment had affected his life since then. "In little ways," said Downing. "For example, I never say 'seven-fifteen' anymore. I say 'quarter after seven.'"

Nineteen eighty was the year George Brett almost hit .400. It was also reliever Dan Quisenberry's second year up with the Royals, and he was very much in awe of his teammate Brett. How did the team get along during Brett's several injuries that season? "Our goal was to get as many rainouts as possible," said Quisenberry.

In 1962 Casey Stengel was the first-ever manager of the expansion New York Mets and surprised everyone by taking catcher Hobie Landrith with his first draft pick. Why? "Because if you don't have a catcher," explained Casey, "you get a lot of passed balls."

Chapter 3

THE COACHES, SCOUTS, AND MANAGERS, PART I

THEY HAD HIM SCOUTED

OK, here's a challenge for you.

Walk down any big-city street and ask the first hundred people you meet what was the highlight of Twins coach Al Newman's big-league career.

The odds are that only if you're lucky enough to run into his mother will anyone give you the right answer. Which is: he hit one homer, in his second season, and then went the remaining six years of his career without hitting another.

Mom might even be able to repeat Newman's excuse for this ignominious feat.

"I just never got my pitch," he explained.

But playing a good game doesn't qualify anybody for inclusion within these hallowed pages.

Talking a good game does.

Carry on . . .

OK, what does a bench coach really do? Don Zimmer gives us an example of how it worked when he was with the Yankees: "If Joe Torre called for a hit-and-run, and it worked, I'd pat him on the back and say, 'Smart move.' If it didn't work, I'd go down and hang around the water cooler."

Ellis Clary played for the old Washington Senators and then coached, managed in the minors, and scouted for the Twins for 40 years. Who was the worst prospect he ever saw? "I once scouted a pitcher who was so bad," said Clary, "that when he came into a game, the grounds crew dragged the warning track."

In the mid-eighties Jackie Moore briefly managed the Oakland A's. Very briefly. So when he was asked whether he considered himself an interim manager, his answer was both correct and prophetic. "In the majors," he said, "all managers are interim."

Pirates manager Bill Virdon was not the excitable type, but he made an exception about a spectacular catch that the Cardinals' Lou Brock made against his Pittsburgh team. "I don't believe it," he said. "Brock could never do that again—not even on instant replay!"

Things did not go well for manager Billy Gardner's Twins in the eighties. Injuries, off years, and pitching problems conspired to keep his team mired deep in the standings. "The way things are going for me," he said, "if I bought a pumpkin farm, they'd cancel Halloween."

Harvey Kuenn's .353 batting average led the American League in 1959, and his .303 lifetime average proved that hitting was no great problem for him. Switching to managing the Milwaukee Brewers proved an easy task, too. "All I do is write their names on the lineup card and let them play," he said. "I haven't misspelled a name yet."

Most big-league managers know that being hired is just the first step toward being fired. (OK, Connie Mack lasted 50 years as manager of the Philadelphia Athletics, but he also owned the team.) Tony LaRussa said, "When I first became a manager, I asked Chuck Tanner for advice. He told me, 'Always rent.'"

The Seattle Mariners finished last in the A.L. West in 1983—again. So when Del Crandall was named manager midway through the season, a local critic had this reaction: "Being named manager of the Seattle Mariners is like being named the head chef at McDonald's."

In the spring of 1986, after 10 years of faithful service, catcher/outfielder John Wathan and the Kansas City Royals cut a deal. At a hastily called press conference, the club announced that right now—as of this moment—Wathan was no longer a player; he was a coach. Wathan then stepped to the microphone and said, "The game has changed a lot since I played."

When the Mets came into existence in 1962, everyone predicted they would finish in last place. And, at 60 games out, the Mets didn't disappoint them. But manager Casey Stengel never gave up. At midseason a reporter asked Stengel where he thought the club would end up. "We will finish," said Casey, checking the schedule, "in Chicago."

In 1980 the San Francisco Giants were stumbling along under .500, and manager Dave Bristol was not happy. "There'll be two buses leaving the hotel for the ballpark tomorrow," he said. "The two o'clock bus will be for those of you who need a little extra work. The empty bus will leave at five o'clock."

Once when Mets manager Yogi Berra brought in reliever Tug McGraw to replace Tom Seaver, he said, "Can you get 'em out?" "Jeez, Yogi," said McGraw, "you just took out the best pitcher in baseball. If he can't get 'em out, what do you expect from me?"

In 1962 Alvin Dark, manager of the Giants, had two major accomplishments: he led his team to the N.L. pennant and he was right on with one prediction. Seeing then-rookie Gaylord Perry flail away in batting practice, he said, "We will have a man on the moon before Perry hits a home run." Seven years later, on July 20, 1969, *Apollo 11* landed on the moon. Thirty-four minutes later Perry hit his first homer.

In 1979 the Yankees got off to a slow start and stumbled to a fourth-place finish. According to manager Bob Lemon, hitting was the problem. "The way we're hitting," he said at one point, "sick people are getting out of bed and wanting to pitch against us."

When Frank Robinson took over the Cleveland Indians in 1975, he became the first black manager in the big leagues. But his reign lasted only two and a half years. Was his problem a lack of communication? "I communicated fine," he said. "The players just didn't like what I had to say."

Chapter 4

THE PLAYERS, PART II

AND THEN CAME THE FIELDING HELMET?

Outfielder Babe Herman was a major contributor to the Dodgers' daffy reputation in the thirties. A big hitter but erratic in the field, he took exception to one reporter's claim that he'd been hit on the head by several fly balls.

"If a ball ever hits me on the head, I'll quit," he said.

"How about on the shoulder?" the reporter asked.

Babe thought for a moment and said, "No, on the shoulder don't count."

Guess that settles that . . .

* * *

The 1930 Philadelphia Phillies were a study in futility, finishing dead last at 40 games out. Their "ace," Claude Willoughby, was 4–17 with a 7.59

ERA and rarely finished a game. Once, when captain Fresco Thompson took the lineup to the ump, the pitcher's slot read, "Willoughby and others."

At the end of the 2002 season, Rickey Henderson had logged 24 seasons in the majors and claimed to be almost 44 years old. A *San Francisco Chronicle* reader disputed that. "Scientists in the Siberian tundra have discovered a perfectly preserved Neolithic hunter," he said, "along with frozen artifacts that include a stone ax and a Rickey Henderson baseball card."

Don Larsen was masterful in his historic and unprecedented perfect game against the Dodgers in the 1956 World Series. Apparently he is also a master of the understatement. When asked how he thought back on the event, he said, "Not many people get to do something that's only been done once."

After the 2000 season, Manny Ramirez left the Indians to sign as a free agent with the Red Sox. At Boston's spring-training camp, the *Miami Herald's* Dan Le Batard questioned Ramirez about a report that because of his base running and fielding lapses, the Indians had tested him for attention deficit disorder. "If they did," said Manny, "I don't remember it."

Shoeless Joe Jackson, of the infamous Chicago Black Sox, was not a scholarly man, and he was a bit sensitive about it. One day a heckler got on him unmercifully, asking Jackson repeatedly if he could spell *illiterate*. In the late innings Jackson slammed a stand-up three bagger and shouted up at the offending man, "Hey, big mouth, can you spell *triple?*"

In 16 years Mark Grace played 2,245 games at first base. And he pitched one inning. Did you know that?

No one has ever accused first baseman Mark Grace of being fleet of foot. Yet one of his early contributions after becoming an Arizona Diamondback was a booming, bases-loaded triple. He said he briefly considered going for an inside-the-park homer, but "then I realized who was running."

When veteran Dodgers reliever Jesse Orosco reported to training camp before the 2001 season, he is said to have asked for 00 as his new uniform number. According to Fox Sports Net's Keith Olbermann, that's because the 44-year-old hurler had been around so long that his odometer had turned over.

45

Pitcher Mickey McDermott was happy when he was traded to the New York Yankees in 1956. Yankees outfielder Hank Bauer was not, however. "This means I don't get to hit against him anymore," he said. "I just lost about 60 points off my batting average."

After the 2000 season, outfielder Juan Gonzalez declined Detroit's seven-year, $140-million offer and signed a one-year deal with Cleveland for $10 million. The *Chicago Tribune*'s Steve Rosenbloom questioned Gonzalez's financial savvy: "The Indians say he passed their physical, but what about the mental?"

When Phillies outfielder Lenny Dykstra retired after the 1996 season, it was pretty obvious that he had modeled himself after Pete Rose: scratching and diving and sliding with reckless abandon. Once, when clubhouse manager Frank Coppenbarger was asked why he had ordered a new load of dirt for Veterans Stadium's infield, he said, "All the old dirt's on Lenny Dykstra's uniform."

When pitcher Clyde "Pea Ridge" Day came to the Dodgers in 1931, he brought a weird habit with him. Whenever he closed an inning with a strikeout, he would stand on the mound, flap his arms, and emit a screeching hog call. Eventually, manager Wilbert Robinson banned Day's act, saying, "A man has no right to be sillier than God intended him to be."

Bob Patterson pitched in the majors, with moderate success, for 13 years. He retired in 1998 with a 39–40 record and a 4.08 ERA. His way with words was above average, however. Asked what he threw on a particular home-run ball, he said, "It was a cross between a screwball and a change-up. I call it a screwup."

Slugger Dave Kingman hit 442 home runs during a 16-year big-league career. Some claim he made that many errors, as well. Broadcaster Richie Ashburn, upon hearing that an equipment man had been called to repair Kingman's glove, said, "They should have called a welder."

One of the characters that populated the expansion New York Mets in the early sixties was tight-lipped catcher Choo Choo Coleman. Desperate to get more than a yes or no out of Coleman, interviewer Ralph Kiner said, "Choo Choo, what's your wife's name and what's she like?" "Her name is Mrs. Coleman," said Choo Choo, "and she likes me."

During their pennant drive in 1987, Twins pitcher Joe Niekro was caught on the mound with an emery board in his pocket. Doctoring the ball? Hardly, said columnist Pat Reusse. Reusse claimed that, between innings, Niekro was finishing off his wood carving of Mother Teresa.

Tommy John, at age 45, didn't seem too concerned about his advancing years when told that his three errors in one inning had just tied the record for pitchers set 90 years earlier by one Cy Seymour. "Good old Cy," he said. "I think I pitched against him once back in the Eastern League."

Jose Rijo, who pitched for the Reds from 1988 through 1995 and then again in 2001 and 2002, learned something from his frequent salary squabbles with Cincinnati management. Asked about his divorce in 1991, he said, "My wife, she takes half of everything. I give up six runs, three are charged to her."

Ron Hunt was a two-time National League All-Star, but he was best known for his uncanny skill at deliberately getting nicked by the pitch. Painlessly, of course. In 1971 he led the league with 50 HBP, while the guy in second place had only 9. The Montreal Expos press guide once summed up his rare talent rather nicely. "Ron gets good skin on the ball," it said.

Chapter 5

THE UMPIRES

BILL KLEM'S ADVICE

Pity the poor umpire. Misunderstood and unloved, the object of derision and scorn, he is pelted with malicious catcalls and other verbal abuse. His honesty and eyesight are repeatedly questioned. All of this is, of course, grossly unfair. The typical umpire is a man of integrity and clear vision, a man of sympathy and compassion.

As an example I give you 36-year National League veteran Bill Klem. Grizzled and hard-bitten, he offered kindly and sage advice to comfort a young pitcher in distress.

Hall of Famer Rogers Hornsby had an infallible eye at the plate. Once, a rookie pitcher faced Hornsby with a 3–0 count, after having complained loudly about the call on each previous pitch. The pitcher then grooved a fastball and Hornsby drove it completely out of sight. As the great man circled the bases, umpire Bill Klem strolled to the mound and said, "Young man, never question a call when Mr. Hornsby is at bat. When the ball is over the plate, Mr. Hornsby will let you know."

For more proof of the umpire's valor and righteous demeanor, please continue.

* * *

When umpire Bill McGowan called a runner out on a close play at second, the guy jumped up and

vehemently protested that he was safe. "You're out," said McGowan, "and if you don't believe it, check tomorrow morning's newspaper."

Say what you like about American League ump Bill Valentine. He was a very sensitive man. Asked why he had ejected manager Alvin Dark in a 1968 game, Valentine said, "I was shocked at the language he used. He suggested there had not been a marriage in my family for three generations."

Was the bad feeling between manager Earl Weaver and umpire Ron Luciano for real? Luciano clarified things a while back. "Earl and I had dinner at 6:30 last Sunday night," said Luciano. "He was in Florida. I was in New York. That's the closest we'll ever get."

Yankees outfielder Lou Piniella once questioned a Steve Palermo call with, "Where was that pitch at?" The umpire responded with, "A man ennobled by the same pinstripes worn by Ruth and Gehrig should know better than to end a sentence with a preposition." "OK," said Piniella, "where was that pitch at, asshole?"

Here's a classic exchange between Hall of Fame catcher Bill Dickey and umpire Beans Reardon, who had just called a pitch a ball during the 1939 World Series.

Dickey: What was wrong with it?

Reardon: Nothin'.

Dickey: It was right down the middle.

Reardon: It was.

Dickey: Why ain't it a strike then?

Reardon: Because I called it a ball.

Dickey: Oh.

Milt Pappas can certainly remember one call he thought was less than perfect.

Crusty old Giants manager John McGraw and crusty old umpire Tim Hurst never got along very well. As Hurst called a ball against an opposition batter, McGraw screamed, "You blind old bat, that split the plate!" When the next pitch was called a strike, McGraw yelled, "The *first* one was better than *that*!" "OK," said Hurst, "ball two!"

Umpire Steve Palermo was seated at the head table at an off-season banquet when he asked the man next to him to pass him another pat of butter. The man said, "One pat of butter, that's the rule." Palermo said, facetiously, "Perhaps you don't know

60

who I am." "Perhaps you don't know who *I* am," the man replied. "I'm the guy in charge of the butter."

A sports official must be in complete control at all times, as highly regarded umpire Bill Guthrie once demonstrated. As a runner slid into third, Guthrie hesitated with his call long enough for the third baseman to yell, "Well, what is he?" "He ain't *nothin'* till I say so," said Guthrie.

Everyone was surprised when, after what seemed to be a quiet discussion of a call at third base, the Pirates' usually mild-mannered Pie Traynor was ejected by umpire Bill Klem. Klem later explained that he had excused Mr. Traynor because he had said he wasn't feeling well. Not feeling well? "Yes," said Klem. "He said he was sick and tired of my stupid decisions."

Plate umpire Jocko Conlan got fed up with Richie Ashburn complaining about his calls, so he told *him* to call the next pitch. Ashburn looked at the next offering and said, tentatively, "Strike?" Conlan said, "Richie, you're the first hitter in history to bat and ump at the same time, and you blew it!"

Orioles manager Earl Weaver and umpire Ron Luciano were constantly at each other's throats. Catcher Elrod Hendricks, an aspiring peacemaker, once tried to explain Weaver to Luciano. "C'mon, Ron, Earl's not so bad," he said. "He's just not happy unless he's not happy."

Umpire Marty Springstead will never forget the first game he worked in 1965. Huge, menacing Frank Howard was at bat when Marty called a strike at the knees. Howard glared and said, "Get one thing straight, Buster. On me, that's no strike!" Next pitch, same place. "Two!" said Springstead. "TWO WHAT!?" roared Howard. "Too low, Frank," said Springstead. "Much too low."

In 1972 Cubs pitcher Milt Pappas was one strike away from a perfect game, but ump Bruce Froemming called a questionable ball to walk a man. Announcer Lou Boudreau later told Froemming that he blew a chance to be the 12th ump in history to call a perfect game. Who was number 11? Boudreau didn't know. "See how famous I would've been?" said Froemming.

Al Barlick, a National League umpire, once made a controversial call against the hometown Reds and was approached the next morning by a fan in the hotel coffee shop. "You really blew that call yesterday," said the man. Barlick, furious, jerked his thumb toward the door and yelled, "Get outta here!" And the man left in a hurry. "It was the first time," said writer Jack Herman, "that an umpire ever threw a fan out of a coffee shop."

Chapter 6

THE HALL OF
FAMERS, PART II

YOU DO
WHAT YOU
GOTTA DO!

When acrobatic shortstop Ozzie Smith was inducted into the Hall of Fame in 2002, his fans recalled, among many others, the double play he turned against the Dodgers 10 years earlier. Lenny Harris had come in high, and the Wizard of Oz (as Smith was affectionately known) had simply gone up over him.

"How?" asked Harris.

"Son," said Ozzie, "you were on the third floor, so I just went up to the sixth."

* * *

Jim Palmer pitched for the Orioles for 19 years and won 268 games. For 14 of those years his manager was Earl Weaver, and theirs was not a happy relationship. Many of their hundreds of arguments involved what Weaver claimed were Palmer's imaginary ailments. Once, stopped on suspicion of drunken driving, Earl was asked if he had any physical problems. "Yes," said Weaver. "Jim Palmer."

In a review of Ernie Banks' 19-year career with the Cubs, someone pointed out that in spite of his 512 home runs, Chicago never won a pennant while he was there, and, in fact, their average finish was sixth place. Longtime player and manager Jimmy Dykes, in defense of finishing sixth, said, "Without Banks the Cubs would have finished in Albuquerque."

Pitcher Satchel Paige always maintained that Cool Papa Bell was the fastest man ever to play the game. How fast? "One time he hit a line drive right past my ear," said Satch. "I turned around and saw the ball hit him in the ass as he slid into second."

Much-traveled catcher
Bob Uecker had heard
all about how tough it was
to play in Philadelphia, but
it wasn't until he was
traded to the Phillies that
he became a believer.
"The cops picked me up
late one night," he said.
"They fined me $100 for
being drunk and $500
for being a Phillie."

With an arsenal consisting of a knuckler and little else, Phil Niekro lasted 24 years in the majors and won 318 games. Former Yankee Bobby Murcer explained why that one pitch was all Mr. Niekro needed. "Hitting Phil Niekro's knuckleball was like trying to eat Jell-O with chopsticks," he said.

Ex-manager Tommy Lasorda doesn't talk too much about his big-league pitching record of 0–4. But when Hall of Famer Whitey Ford, who won 236 games, needled Tommy about it, Lasorda asked Ford how many *he* had lost. Whitey said he'd lost 106. "Well, that's 102 more than *I* lost, pal!" said Lasorda.

Leo Durocher survived in the majors for 17 years on his fielding and his bravado, and in spite of his skimpy .247 batting average. In his first couple of years he tried switch-hitting, which prompted a scout to say, "The kid'll hit .400 for you—.200 right-handed and .200 left-handed."

Hall of Fame third baseman Pie Traynor once had to sit out for a few games and suffer while a rookie sub committed error after error. Rushed back into the lineup, Traynor booted the first ball that came to him. "That kid's got third base so screwed up," he grumbled, "that *nobody* can play it."

Catfish Hunter and Reggie Jackson, an opinionated pair, formed an uneasy truce when they both played for the Yankees, but with mixed feelings about each other. "Reggie's really a good guy," Hunter once said. "He'd give you the shirt off his back. Of course, he'd call a press conference to announce it."

Rube Waddell won 27 games for the old Philadelphia Athletics in 1905 and went on to win almost 200 games in the major leagues. According to Mike Royko of the *Chicago Sun-Times*, Rube loved pitching, fishing, and drinking. "When he died," said Royko, "they found him in a gin-filled bathtub with three drunken trout."

In 1971 Major League Baseball named the venerable Satchel Paige to a new wing in the Baseball Hall of Fame—the one for Negro Leagues players. Paige was not impressed. "All they've done," he said, "is to turn Satch from a second-class citizen into a second-class immortal."

When Neil Armstrong first landed on the moon he was puzzled by an unidentifiable white object. Old Yankees hurler Lefty Gomez knew what it was. "It was a home-run ball Jimmy Foxx hit off me in 1937," he said.

This one means absolutely nothing, but that's OK because Casey Stengel said it. "There comes a time in every man's life," he said, "and I've had plenty of them."

Reggie Jackson had such success in the postseason playoffs and in the World Series that he became known as Mr. October. So was there any downside to playing in the fall classic? "The only reason I didn't like playing in the World Series," he said, "was that I couldn't watch myself play."

In Don Drysdale's 14 years with the Dodgers he chalked up more than 200 wins and made the National League All-Star team eight times. Not the least of the tools contributing to his success was intimidation. He did not hesitate to back a hitter off the plate and, in fact, his stats included 154 hit batsmen. "If the hitter is timid," he once said, "the pitcher has to remind him he's timid."

Chapter 7

THE COACHES,
SCOUTS, AND
MANAGERS, PART II

A TIP
FROM CASEY

Casey Stengel was forever drawing on his vast experience to advise young players.

Once, when one of his Mets pitchers committed a balk because a fly landed on his nose, Casey strolled to the mound and said, "Son, if you want to pitch in the majors, you're going to have to learn to catch those in your mouth."

Another time, at a tryout camp, Casey noticed a young prospect taking infield practice wearing shin guards. Casey asked if he was also a catcher.

"No," said the boy, "I'm just a little weak on ground balls."

* * *

Joe Torre never played for Tommy Lasorda, but sharing Lasorda's Italian heritage, he is presumed to know all about Tommy's eating habits. Is it true that

> **Casey Stengel knew why his Mets lost 120 games in 1962: "It ain't sex that ruins 'em. It's stayin' up all night looking for it."**

Lasorda concentrates on spaghetti, meatballs, and sausage? "Tommy will eat anything," said Torre, "as long as you pay for it."

When Bobby Valentine managed the Rangers, he greatly admired Don Baylor. Because he was tough. Because he was built like a tank. Because he never gave a pitcher the satisfaction of backing away from an inside pitch. "Why should he?" said Valentine. "That's like a car swerving to avoid a squirrel."

Indians slugger Rocky Colavito was having a bad year in 1959 and was unhappy about it. The trade rumors he heard made it even worse, so manager Joe Gordon tried to help. "Rocky, I absolutely will not trade you," he said. Then he added, "But if you don't start hitting, I'm sending you down to Reading."

In 1985, the final year of the nine that Chuck Tanner managed the Pittsburgh Pirates, they finished in last place, 43½ games out of first. But he still maintained his characteristic optimistic attitude. "If I were the captain of the *Titanic*," he said, "I would tell my passengers we were just stopping for ice."

Ellis Clary played for the Washington Senators for a few years and then spent 40 years scouting for the team after it moved to the Twin Cities and became the Twins. At that point he abruptly quit and started scouting for the White Sox. Why? "I change jobs *every* 40 years," he explained.

Chicago Cub Joe Pepitone was on third base and looked to manager Leo Durocher in the dugout for a sign. To confirm the sign, third-base coach

Joey Amalfitano winked at Pepitone. In response to the wink, Pepitone blew a kiss at Amalfitano and, as he did so, got picked off. Durocher was not pleased.

In the middle of the 1985 season, the Twins fired manager Billy Gardner and replaced him with Ray Miller. In his exit press conference, Gardner was asked if he had any advice for Twins management. "If they wanted my advice, they wouldn't have fired me," he said.

Longtime manager and coach Charlie Dressen had no peer in the fine art of stealing other teams' signals. In a pregame meeting when he managed the 1953 National League All-Stars, a player asked about the signs to be used. "Don't worry about it," said Dressen. "I'll give each of you the ones your own team uses during the season."

Losing baseball managers have been routinely fired just for losing. But way back in 1892, Washington Senators skipper Bill Barney was axed for—insubordination? "We asked him to resign and he refused," said owner Earl Wagner. "Insubordination."

When you'd been around as long as Casey Stengel, you covered all the angles. "Before I released a guy, I always had his room searched for a gun," he said. "You couldn't take chances with some of those birds."

During his eight years in the American League, Bo Jackson made a pretty good run at equaling his football accomplishments. Prodigious home runs were his specialty. After one monstrous 515 footer, coach Bob Schaefer was asked what Bo had hit. "I think it was a Top-Flite," said Schaefer.

Chapter 8

HITTING AHEAD OF THE LEADOFF MAN?

With his eight-year lifetime average of .210, infielder Steve Jeltz did not strike fear into the hearts of pitchers. In fact, in 1989, even with no DH, Phillies manager Nick Leyva once had Jeltz bat ninth in the order—behind the pitcher.

Why ninth?

"Because there is no tenth," said Leyva.

* * *

First baseman Rudy York may have kicked a few grounders in his 13-year stint in the majors, but he hit a ton of home runs and hated to be accused of anything dumb. He once awoke to find his hotel bed on fire. Had he been smoking? "No, no," he said. "The bed was already on fire when I laid down."

91

Charlie Lau caught such knuckleball artists as Hoyt Wilhelm and Phil Niekro, so he had plenty of chances to see hitters flail away at the dancing deliveries. And to try to catch them himself. "There are two theories on catching the knuckleball," said Lau. "Unfortunately, neither of them works."

Pitcher Mark Knudson had a so-so eight-year career with the Astros, the Brewers, and the Rockies. He had close to a .500 winning percentage and fairly good control. But once, finding himself with three men on, he proceeded to throw two wild pitches that allowed all three runners to score. "That's one way to pitch out of a bases-loaded situation," said Milwaukee manager Tom Trebelhorn.

In the first inning of Game 2 of the 1984 World Series, the first three Detroit Tigers each ripped the first pitch for a hit. At that point, Padres catcher Terry Kennedy said he considered calling for a pitchout just so he could handle the ball.

Catcher Doug Gwosdz lasted only a few years with the San Diego Padres, but the most memorable thing about those years is not his statistics. It's the nickname he was tagged with: Eye Chart.

Carl Furillo spent 15 years as an outfielder with the Dodgers, and his .299 lifetime batting average fell just short of his .300 goal. To what does he attribute his near miss? "Carrots were good for my eyes," he said, "but they didn't straighten out the curveball."

Pitcher Bryan Harvey may have decided to do a little editing on his California scoreboard bio in 1992. One line read, "Life ambition: To end all the killing in the world." The next line said, "Hobbies: Hunting and fishing."

Willy Miranda, who set the standard for batting futility by hitting a paltry .159 in 1959 and finishing with a career batting average of just .221, considered it an affectation for hitters (especially weak hitters) to wear batting gloves. "How's a guy gonna get blisters hittin' .170?" he asked.

Catcher Bob Uecker's biggest talent was putting the best possible spin on just about everything. When he hit his first home run in 1962, he said, "Between me and my roommate, Eddie Matthews, we've now hit 400 homers."

Mike Flanagan pitched in the American League for 18 years and vowed he'd never play for a New York team. Why? "The first time I ever played there with the Orioles, I got into the bullpen car and they told me to lock the doors."

Just prior to the 2000 season, the Tampa Bay Devil Rays acquired Vinny Castilla and Greg Vaughn

94

for a team that already had Jose Canseco and Fred McGriff. During the previous season, those four accounted for 454 strikeouts. "Which means," said the *Baltimore Sun*'s Peter Schmuck, "that the Rays should save a little on air-conditioning."

It was during his fifth year in the majors that catcher Jim Essian hit his first home run. And it was a big occasion. "I wanted to go into my home-run trot," he said, "but then I realized I didn't have one."

In the mid-eighties Twins stopper Ron Davis objected to a newspaper story saying he was critical of management trading away several of the team's key players. "All I said was that the trades were dumb and stupid," he said, "and they took that and blew it all out of proportion."

> With all those World Series wins over Brooklyn, Whitey Ford probably helped keep Carl Furillo's career average under .300.

When Joe Garagiola was playing, it wasn't a good idea to try to psych him out. He knew all the tricks. One example: "Never trust a base runner who's limping. A guy gets a hit behind him and he'll take off like he just got back from Lourdes."

Third baseman Vance Law's lifetime batting average of .256 would indicate that he probably had a few slumps in his time. This description would indicate that he didn't enjoy them: "When you're in a slump, it's like looking out at the field and seeing one big glove."

Pitcher Joaquin Andujar's 13-year career featured one year with 20 victories and one incredibly insightful bit of philosophy. "When it comes to baseball," he said, "you never know."

How tough are the fans in Philadelphia? Former Phillies catcher Bob Uecker has been there and he knows. "One Easter Sunday the players had an Easter-egg hunt at the ballpark for their children," he said, "and the fans booed the kids who didn't find any."

Before the 1985 season the Cardinals traded shortstop Jose Gonzalez to the Giants. Then, for his own reasons, Jose changed his name to Uribe Gonzalez and, later in the season, changed it to Jose Uribe. Giants coach Rocky Bridges nailed it when he said, "Jose was the first player in a trade to *really* be named later."

Dave Parker was a big, strong outfielder who played for 19 years and always put up big numbers—

including those on the bathroom scale. Late in his career his weight problem became so obvious that a popular joke was, "Dave has gotten so fat he's taking his showers in a car wash."

Left-hander John Tudor got off to a terrible start with the Cardinals in 1985, but then things got squared away. In midseason a reader wrote to *The Sporting News* to say that "Tudor would be having a good year if it weren't for April and May." To which another writer responded, "That's like saying that if it weren't for WWI and WWII, Germany would be having a great century."

In June of 1985 Mets pitcher Bruce Berenyi had some arm trouble and was told to visit Dr. James Andrews in Columbus, Georgia. Being a resourceful fellow, Bruce made his own reservations and flew to Columbus. Unfortunately, the Columbus he flew to was in Ohio.

Chapter 9

THE OWNERS
AND OFFICIALS

THE
CUSTOMER
IS KING

Owners and general managers take a lot of heat from fans, players, and the press.

George "the Boss" Steinbrenner is too . . . well, bossy. Calvin Griffith of the Senators and Twins was too cheap. Charlie Finley was too egotistical. Ted Turner is too political.

And then there was Bill Veeck. Veeck, who at various times owned the Indians, Browns, and White Sox and who died in 1986, had only one group of detractors: other owners.

He was imaginative, fun-loving, generous, promotion-minded, and, perhaps most of all, flexible.

The St. Louis Browns were consistent when Bill Veeck owned them in the early fifties: they were always near the bottom, both in the standings and in attendance. Veeck once invited a friend to a game. "Maybe I'll do it," the man said. "What time does the game start?"

"What time would be convenient for you?" Veeck asked.

Let's check out a few more of the moguls . . .

*   *   *

Philadelphia pitcher Rube Waddell was having a great year in 1905 and liked to celebrate each victory. After one win, a detective hauled a wobbly Waddell into the A's hotel and told manager Connie Mack that he was tossing Waddell into jail unless Mack put up a drunkenness fine of $10 (big bucks in those days). An hour after posting the fine, Mack, passing a saloon, looked in to see Waddell and the "detective" drinking up Mack's $10.

As general manager of the Cardinals and then the Dodgers, Branch Rickey had a reputation as the wiliest trader and smartest dealer in baseball history.

104

Veteran catcher and manager Paul Richards agreed: "Rickey's a guy who'll go into a revolving door in the section behind you and come out in front of you."

When Gene Autry and Walter O'Malley were the owners of, respectively, the Angels and the Dodgers, they were not exactly pals. Autry explained: "There's nothing in the world I wouldn't do for him and there's nothing in the world he wouldn't do for me. And that's the way it is . . . we go through life doing nothing for each other."

When the Arizona Diamondbacks visited the White House after winning the 2001 World Series, general manager Joe Garagiola Jr. came along. President George W. Bush, former owner of the

Texas Rangers and longtime baseball fan, knew all about Joe's father, who caught for the Cardinals and others. What did the president think of Joe Jr.? "I'm always suspicious of guys with famous fathers," he said.

The players and their union don't have a high opinion of management's intellect. During the last strike, one of the players' lawyers said, "What the Baseball Players Association doesn't realize is that in these negotiations, they are dealing with some of the greatest minds of the 12th century."

When Commissioner Bud Selig made the argument to contract the Montreal Expos before the 2002 season, he cited the team's lowly attendance figures as one of the reasons. The *Toronto Sun*'s Bill Lankhof agreed. "Montreal is the only major league city where instead of announcing the starting lineups," he said, "they introduce the entire crowd."

Could baseball's star wheeler-dealers transfer their skills to other fields? White Sox GM Frank Lane thought so. In 1955 Lane said he had the solution to all our Cold War problems: "Just sit Molotov down between Branch Rickey and Casey Stengel," he said, "and in four years Russia will have nothing left but Siberia and a couple of left-handed pitchers."

Twins owner Calvin Griffith had plenty of baseball smarts, but he was a little shaky on his vocabulary. Discussing Cardinals pitcher John Tudor going into the 1987 Series, Griffith said, "Tudor's good, but the Twins should hit him. He's not that overbearing."

The day after Bill Veeck used Eddie Gaedel, the famous 3'7" midget pinch-hitter, the American League banned all midgets. Veeck immediately demanded a ruling on whether Phil Rizzuto, the Yankees' 5'6" shortstop, was a short ballplayer or a tall midget.

George Steinbrenner has owned the Yankees for more than 20 years. From firing managers to buying championships to having disputes with other owners, controversy has never been far away. One of those other owners, the White Sox's Jerry Reinsdorf, is not a Steinbrenner fan. "I can tell when George is lying," he said. "His lips move."

Branch Rickey was
often described as
the shrewdest trader,
the sharpest negotiator, the
smartest man in baseball.
Sportswriter Red Smith,
however, did not hold a
very high opinion of the
intellectual prowess of
baseball management. "To
call Branch Rickey the
smartest man in baseball,"
he said, "is to damn with
the faintest of praise."

Frustrated because his Boston Braves had lost
103 games in 1928, the owner, Judge Emil Fuchs,
appointed himself manager for 1929. The judge was
not a baseball man, but he was firm. Veteran third
baseman Joe Dugan, unhappy when Fuchs asked
him to play shortstop, said, "Where is shortstop on

this field?" Fuchs fumed and said to a nearby player, "Show Mr. Dugan where the clubhouse is and how to take off his uniform."

When Edward Bennett Williams owned the Baltimore Orioles, he was frustrated with the conservative nature of his counterparts in the other league. "National League owners are 100 percent against change," he said. "I think it was a long time before any of them had indoor plumbing."

Bill Veeck must be twirling in his grave with the way players' salaries have escalated. Back when all the inflation started, Bill was heard to lament, "I don't mind the high price of stardom, but I *don't* like the high price of mediocrity."

After negotiating his 1945 contract, second baseman Eddie Stanky joined the throng who considered Dodgers GM Branch Rickey the toughest man to deal with in all of baseball. "I got a very small raise and a million dollars worth of free advice," he said.

Charles O. Finley (the *O* was for *owner*) put together some formidable teams during the 12 years he was at the helm of the Oakland A's. But he didn't pick up many admirers along the way. *L.A. Times* columnist Jim Murray was one of his detractors. "Finley is a self-made man who worships his creator," wrote Murray.

Gene Mauch managed Gene Autry's Angels for five seasons, so he got to know "the Cowboy" pretty well. Did Autry have a passion for winning? "Mr. Autry's favorite horse was named Champion," said Mauch. "He ain't never had a horse called Runner-Up."

It was a case of telegram tag. When a Cleveland outfielder rejected a contract offer by returning the document unsigned, Indians GM Hank Greenberg wired, "In your haste to accept terms, you neglected to sign contract." The player wired back, "In your haste to give me a raise, you put in the wrong figure."

Brooklyn general manager Branch Rickey once decreed that long-distance phone calls were too expensive and all farm-club communications had to be 10 words or fewer by telegram. So in response to Rickey's wire asking Fort Worth's Bobby Bragan, "Do you need shortstop or is present one OK?" Bragan wired, "Yes." Rickey wired, "Yes, what?" Bragan wired, "Yes, sir."

During the mid-seventies and early eighties the Twins usually finished in the middle of the A.L. West pack, but they were always right up there in home runs allowed. "The fans like to see home runs," said VP Clark Griffith, "and we've assembled a pitching staff for their enjoyment."

Superpromoter Bill Veeck was not all fun and frolic; he had some deep insights into the game. "Baseball is almost the only orderly thing in a very disorderly world," he once said. "If you get three strikes, the best lawyer in the universe can't get you off."

After the 1952 season, slugger Ralph Kiner argued with Branch Rickey, GM of the last-place

Pirates, over a proposed 25 percent pay cut. Kiner pointed out that he had led the league in homers for seven straight years. Rickey's response: "We could have finished last without you."

Chapter 10

The Hall of

Famers, Part III

Hazardous
Duty

Catcher Bob Uecker and pitcher Phil Niekro were teammates for a half season with Atlanta in 1967. Chasing down Niekro's elusive knucklers for half a season was enough for Uecker.

After one game GM Paul Richards disagreed when the trainer said Niekro could throw again the next day.

"Why?" asked the trainer. "You think he needs more rest?"

"No," said Richards. "Uecker needs more rest."

*   *   *

During the 1911 season, the year Ty Cobb hit .420, a local amateur pitcher told Tigers manager Hughie Jennings that he could strike Cobb out on three pitches. The test was set up and the young

119

man threw three pitches. Cobb hit two out of the park and hit the right-center-field wall with the third. "Well?" said Jennings. "Are you sure that's Ty Cobb in there?" asked the kid.

When Casey Stengel took over the expansion New York Mets, he'd already managed for more than 20 years and had few illusions left. In a pregame review of one day's opposing lineup, he came to the name of Giants slugger Willie McCovey and, turning to pitcher Roger Craig, said, "Tell me, Mr. Craig, how are we going to defense Mr. McCovey today—in the lower deck or the upper deck?"

What can one famous pitcher teach another of the following generation? When Nolan Ryan asked Satchel Paige what his most effective pitch was, Satch told him, "The bow-tie pitch." Is that a fastball? "It's a fastball," said Satch, "right up here," as he drew his finger across his neck.

Tommy Lasorda does tend to exaggerate a bit, but—well, you decide. At midseason one year his Dodgers' lineup was so decimated by injuries that he said he called the suicide hotline for help. "When I explained the situation, they told me to go ahead—I'd be doing the right thing."

Even though he was eventually inducted into the Hall of Fame, Ernie Lombardi came to be the prototypical catcher: big and slow. Ernie was once described as having been thrown out at first trying to stretch a double into a single. Joe Garagiola, a catcher himself, said that the wind always seems to blow against catchers when they are running.

With the terrifying speed of his pitches, Nolan Ryan led his league in strikeouts 11 times. In his first few seasons, however, his lack of control was terrifying, too. Oscar Gamble spoke for many hitters during that time when he said, "A good night against Ryan is when you go 0-for-4 and don't get hit in the head."

When Frank Robinson joined Brooks Robinson on the Orioles in 1966, the pair immediately led the team to the pennant. One infielder, one outfielder. One black, one white. Two Robinsons. To clarify things for newsmen, Frank explained, "There should be no confusion. Can't you see we wear different numbers?"

One of Joe DiMaggio's less memorable World Series moments invited a comparison to a chimney sweep.

Rogers Hornsby's .358 lifetime batting average is second only to Ty Cobb's .367, and outside of hitting, he had no other hobbies. What about golf? "When I hit a ball," said Hornsby, "I want someone else to go chase it."

During one game against the Blue Jays, Kansas City's George Brett hit an almost certain triple into his own bullpen, but Royals reliever Mike Armstrong, warming up there and thinking it was foul, fielded it. So the ump stopped a very unhappy Brett at second base. Armstrong, by way of smoothing things over, said, "I told George I would have thrown him out at third anyway."

Was Babe Ruth the king of New York during his heyday? Consider this: he was once stopped by a cop who told him he was driving the wrong way—that this was a one-way street. Ruth: "I'm only *drivin'* one way!" He beat the rap.

In the World Series of 1949, the Yankees beat the Dodgers four games to one. During one of the games, Joe DiMaggio went 0-for-4, striking out twice and hitting two straight pop-ups. Columnist Bugs Baer summarized: "Yesterday, DiMaggio could have done all his hitting in a chimney."

Hall of Fame outfielder Paul Waner spent most of his 20-year career with the Pittsburgh Pirates and, in spite of his debilitating hobbies, managed a .333

lifetime batting average. Those pastimes—drinking and staying out late—also kept him broke much of the time. "They say money talks," he once said, "but the only thing it ever says to me is 'good-bye.'"

Hack Wilson led the N.L. in home runs four times and, in 1930, set the all-time RBI record with 191. According to some authorities, he also usually led the league in booze consumption. "Hack was built along the lines of a beer keg," said writer Shirley Povich, "and was not unfamiliar with its contents."

Hall of Fame catcher Bill Dickey's memory of opposing batters was phenomenal. Joe Gantenbein, a utility infielder who played briefly with the Philadelphia A's in 1939 and 1940, approached Dickey at a hotel during the 1943 World Series and asked if Dickey remembered him. "I don't recall your name," said Dickey, "but when you were with the A's we'd pitch you high and inside. If we pitched you outside, wham! It was the ballgame."

There may have been those among his critics who periodically doubted his sincerity, but no one ever questioned Tom Seaver's desire to win. Across his 20-year career, Tom Terrific posted 311 wins and once said, "There are only two places to be at the end of the year: first place or no place."

Right-handed pull hitter Gary Carter hit 324 homers during his 19 years in the majors, but not many of them were to right field. After one such event he was asked how many *had* been opposite-field blasts. "I can count 'em on the fingers of one hand," said Carter. "Probably 10, at the most."

White Sox catcher Carlton Fisk was an All-Star in 1991, at age 43. Second baseman Steve Lyons thought that Fisk was a phenomenon when they were teammates the year before, and Fisk was a mere 42. "Pudge is so old," Lyons said, "that when he was in school, they didn't have history class."

Mean and nasty pitcher Early Wynn would tolerate no theatrics from the hitters he faced. So how would he deal with today's home-run curtain calls? "All that jumpin' around and tipping their hats, I'd knock 'em all down," he said. "But I wouldn't waste a pitch; I'd hit 'em right in the dugout."

When the L.A. Dodgers swept the Yankees in the 1963 World Series, Sandy Koufax won two of the games, striking out 23 and allowing only three runs and 12 hits in 18 innings. Was Yankees catcher Yogi Berra impressed? "I can see how he won 25 games during the season," said Yogi. "What I don't understand is how he lost 5."

When Hank Aaron homered and singled in his first two at-bats in a game against the Pirates, pitcher Bruce Kison took personal offense. So he knocked Aaron down his next three times at the plate. "I had good luck with him after that," said Kison.

Lefty Gomez's frequent claims about being a terrible hitter are fully supported by his paltry lifetime batting average of .147. He liked to *look* like a hitter, however: adjusting his cap and belt and knocking the dirt from his spikes. Once, though, he missed the spikes, smashed his ankle, and spent three days in the hospital.

Babe Ruth and pitcher Waite Hoyt were more than just teammates on the Yankees; they were drinking buddies. Years later when Hoyt, then a Cincinnati broadcaster, disappeared for a few days with what management called amnesia, he got a telegram from the Babe. "Heard about your case of amnesia," it read. "Must be a new brand."

Even when the great Dizzy Dean was at his best, the Giants' Bill Terry hit him like he owned him. In one game, after Terry had sent three straight liners screaming past Dean's head, third baseman Pepper Martin strolled to the mound and said, "Jerome, I don't think you're playin' Terry deep enough."

Chapter 11

THE SHOWBIZ FOLKS

THE TONIGHT SHOW WITH JOHNNY CARSON

Is baseball a regular business or is it show business?

If sixties-era catcher Bob Uecker is our model, the answer is obvious. Stuck with limited talent and an anemic .200 lifetime batting average, the self-deprecating Uecker survived on his ability to keep things light in the clubhouse. He was fun to have around.

Since then he has thrived by keeping things light on the talk-show circuit.

Once, on *The Tonight Show* with Johnny Carson, Uecker spoke of the major role he had played in the 1964 Cardinals' pennant drive—how sitting out much of the season with hepatitis had contributed to their success.

Carson: "How did you catch the hepatitis?"

Uecker: "The trainer injected me with it."

And then there was the time that . . .

An accomplished jazz guitarist as well as an All-Star, New York's Bernie Williams is a frequent guest on late-night television.

Comedian Woody Allen's hang-ups go all the way back to the stickball games of his youth. "I was pretty fast, so sometimes I'd steal second," he said. "But then I'd feel guilty and go back to first."

In 2001 the Utah Supreme Court ruled that grabbing one's crotch in public is against the law. *Tonight Show* host Jay Leno put it into perspective: "There go the Mormons' hopes for ever getting a big-league baseball team in Salt Lake City."

When Elton John announced that he would have laser eye surgery in early 2003, there was speculation about what he would do with his four thousand pairs of glasses. Comedian Jerry Perisho guessed that he'd either give them to a museum or offer them to the Major League Umpires Association.

Craig Kilborn of CBS's *The Late Late Show* won't commit himself on whether Pete Rose should be admitted to baseball's Hall of Fame, but he offers an interesting parallel. "When 87-year-old Raggedy Ann was inducted into the National Toy Hall of Fame, her brother Raggedy Andy was not. Mainly," he said, "because he once bet on a game of Chutes and Ladders."

It's all a matter of priorities. New York restaurateur Toots Shor was chatting with the world-renowned discoverer of penicillin, Sir Alexander

Fleming, when former New York Giants outfielder Mel Ott came through the front door. "Excuse me," said Shor, "somebody important just came in."

First baseman Johnny Mize was a great hitter, but his fielding left a lot to be desired. In fact, when Mize was with the Giants, writer Goodman Ace once sent a wire to manager Leo Durocher that read, "Before each game an announcement says that anyone interfering with or touching a batted ball will be ejected from the park. Please advise Mr. Mize that this does not apply to him."

Because the 2000 World Series featured the Yankees and the Mets and therefore was played entirely in New York, each team saved about $200,000 in travel expenses. "Which," said TV host Conan O'Brien, "in stadium dollars amounts to about two hot dogs and four beers."

George Steinbrenner has settled down a little, but during his earlier years as the Yankees owner, the team's manager job was like a revolving door. Comedian Johnny Carson said it pretty well back then: "There are 11 million unemployed in this country and half of them are ex–Yankee managers."

Among actress Tallulah Bankhead's gifts was her ability to recognize talent. "There have been only two authentic geniuses in the world," she said. "Willie Shakespeare and Willie Mays."

David Letterman may be a Yankees fan, but apparently he didn't think much of Phil Rizzuto, their former announcer. Letterman reported on a man being revived after being technically dead for almost five minutes. What was it like being dead? The man said it was like listening to Phil Rizzuto during a rain delay.

Chapter 12

CALORIES? WHO'S COUNTING?

Mickey Lolich won more than 200 games during 13 years with the Tigers. And, tipping the scales at well over a paunchy 200 pounds, he considered himself something of a role model.

"All the fat guys watch me and say to their wives, 'See, there's a fat guy doing OK. Bring me another beer.'"

*   *   *

Outfielder Richie Scheinblum started his career with the Indians and didn't like it there. "The only good thing about playing in Cleveland," he said, "is that you don't have to go there on road trips."

Pitcher Allie Reynolds started his career in Cleveland and *did* like it there. But they traded him

145

to New York, which he *didn't* like. The Yankees were OK, but he couldn't stand living in Manhattan. "The Indians who sold that island for 24 bucks made a helluva good deal," he said.

Clay Carroll pitched for five different teams, in both leagues, over a 15-year period. So he had a pretty good book on most of the hitters. Languages were another matter, however. While with the Reds, he once asked Pedro Borbon, "Hey, Pedro, how do you say adios in Spanish?"

At an age when all but a few major leaguers are *ex*–major leaguers, Pete Rose was still running to first on a walk and sliding into bases headfirst. During the 1982 season someone commented to Rose that he sure didn't *act* like a 40-year-old. "That's because I'm 41," he said.

In 1981 the Red Sox's Pawtucket farm team was involved in what was at the time the longest game in professional baseball history: 33 innings, lasting eight hours and 25 minutes. It included a couple of third basemen you may have heard of: Cal Ripken Jr. and Wade Boggs. Said Boggs, "In a game like this you can have a bad week in one night."

Pitcher Bob Miller (the left-hander, not either of the two right-handed Bob Millers) finished his short and undistinguished career with the Mets in 1962. But it wasn't his lifetime 6–8 record that did him in. He retired because he "got tired of ducking line drives and backing up home plate."

White Sox outfielder Ron Kittle, with his skimpy .239 lifetime batting average, was never considered a tough out. But he was not easy to pin down in real life. Some relatives were once trying to get him to commit to abandoning the bachelor life. "I'll get married when I get back from St. Louis," he said. "Oh, and when are you going to St. Louis?" asked one. "I'm not," said Kittle.

Padres center fielder Bobby Brown was doing poorly at the plate in the 1984 World Series against the Tigers. And he'd made several crucial errors, as well. So after Game 5, during which his key base hit triggered some Padres activity, writer Pat Reusse said, "That was not the first rally Brown has started in this Series. It's the first one he's started for his own *team*, however."

148

Cubs left-hander Larry French had an All-Star year in 1940, but he was getting bombed during one game against Pittsburgh. At one point, with the bases full, he said, "I stepped off the mound and looked around and there were so many Pirates out there, I thought maybe I was pitching for *them*."

George Strickland was a good-field, no-hit infielder during his 10 years in the majors, but he had a talent for one-liners. During one at-bat, after complaining throughout the game about low pitches being called strikes, he turned back toward the dugout as the ump said, "Hold it, that's only two strikes." "I know," said Strickland, "I brought the wrong club. I'm going back for my wedge."

While pitcher Bill Caudill sat at home, he was traded to the Yankees, who immediately traded him to the Cubs. His reaction? "When I retire," he said, "I'm going to ask the Yankees to send me a uniform with one pinstripe on it."

Playing mainly in the fifties, infielder Rocky Bridges was on seven different teams in 11 years. He claimed that whenever his wife needed to know where he was, she had to call Commissioner Ford Frick. "I *was* in Cincinnati for four years," he said. "But then it took me that long to learn how to spell it."

In 1970 Dodgers infielder Billy Grabarkewitz struck out 149 times. (Babe Ruth's highest season total was 93.) When he was complimented the following spring on making better contact, he shrugged it off with, "I'm just off to a slow start."

Much-traveled reliever Mark Davis spent his first two years (1980–81) with the Phillies, and 12 years later returned there. Rough-hewn first baseman John Kruk pulled no punches as the rewelcoming committee: "Davis can pitch when he's relaxed, and he'll be relaxed here," he said. "And if he isn't, we'll kill him."

Pitcher Mark Fidrych was briefly famous with the Tigers, not for his won-lost record but for his strange antics on the mound—like talking to the ball. Cuban-born Mike Cuellar, nearing the end of his career, decided to try some of Fidrych's conversational tricks, but to no avail. "I talked to the ball in Spanish," he said, "but it was an American ball."

Scott Ostler of the *San Francisco Chronicle* always enjoyed Rickey Henderson's springtime routine: "Rickey always reported to camp about a week late," Ostler said, "sauntered out of the clubhouse about noon, and then, if he saw his shadow, there would be another six weeks of bitching about his contract."

Outfielder Dave Parker won a couple of batting titles during his 11 years with the Pirates, but he never really endeared himself to the fans there. "Dave Parker was so unpopular in Pittsburgh," said sportswriter Charley Feeney, "that he could run for mayor unopposed and still lose."

When Luis Polonia came from the Yankees to the Angels in 1990, Angels infielder Donnie Hill gave him his No. 22. Just being a good guy? "Luis had about $50,000 worth of jewelry with that number on it," said Hill. "I had to either give up the number or buy all his jewelry."

Luis was not happy about the way he'd been used as a pinch-hitter in New York. "The Yankees are interested in only one thing," he said, "and I don't know what it is."

In 1985 Mets pitcher Dwight Gooden had a phenomenal 24–4 record and won the National League Cy Young Award. But the Mets finished three games behind the Cardinals, and outfielder Darryl Strawberry blamed it all on Gooden. "If he hadn't lost those four games," he said, "we win the pennant!"

In 1986 Giants outfielder Jeff Leonard announced that henceforth he was to be called Jeffrey, because it sounded more formal. The writers decided they would help by making his *nickname* more formal, too. They changed it from "Penitentiary Face" to "Correctional Institution Face."

Outfielder Tito Fuentes was not a detail guy. During one series his San Francisco Giants had with the rival L.A. Dodgers, things got a bit heated and some batters were being knocked down. "They shouldn't throw at me," said Fuentes. "I've got five kids. Maybe six."

In 1989 and 1990 promising pitcher Willie Smith didn't live up to his potential with either the Pirates or the Yankees because of wildness. His interviews were on the wild side, too. Asked how big his high school was, he said, "Three stories."

When reliever Doug Jones pitched at Oakland in 2000, it was his seventh team in 16 years. How did he explain his moderate success without ever having a big-league fastball? "My father told me that the faster you throw the ball, the less time you have to duck," he said.

In the mid-eighties Kansas City first baseman Steve Balboni hit a grand slam and said, "This is my first grand slam and I'll never forget it." Reminded that he had also hit one two years earlier, Balboni said, "Oh, yeah, I forgot about that one."

Did Pete Rose really deserve that "Charley Hustle" nickname? Take it from Hank Aaron. "Before the All-Star Game Pete came into the clubhouse and took off his shoes," he said, "and they ran another mile without him."

Some of Mark McGwire's shots were out-of-sight far. And some were straight-up far. Randy Bonferraro described one he saw in St. Louis: "Mark McGwire hit a pop-up so high that all nine guys called for it," he said.

Chapter 13

THE ANNOUNCERS

WHAT'S IN A NAME?

What a cushy job baseball's TV and radio announcers have. They just sit there watching America's favorite sport and talk about it. And they get *paid* for doing it. But take it from the late Tony Conigliaro, the announcer's job is not all wine and roses.

During his playing days Tony had taken some heat from Red Sox fans who felt that he never quite lived up to his potential as a hitter. But that was nothing compared to the flak he took after switching to the broadcast booth.

One critic said, "Tony Conigliaro can't even pronounce his own name."

To which Tony responded, "Well, it's a tough name."

Read on . . .

According to *Sports Illustrated*'s Rick Reilly, announcer Jack Buck had a story for every occasion. "For example," says Reilly, "if an Italian woman were being honored at a banquet, Buck might say, 'I've always had a fondness for Italian women. In fact, during WWII an Italian woman hid me in her basement for three months. [Pause] Of course, this was in Cleveland.'"

Hall of Fame baseball announcer Mel Allen was popular with the ladies, but he never married. Some say it was because he lived at home and his mother was a severe critic of all his female friends. Once, when he entered a restaurant with a stunning young lady, sportswriter Tom Meany said, "Here comes Mel Allen with the future Mrs. Jones."

Former Angels owner Gene Autry was always a bit critical of Howard Cosell's skills as a baseball announcer. "Howard calls a good game," he once said. "It's just not the one you're watching."

In Boston, radio announcer Andy Moss once bemoaned the steadily rising costs at the concession stands. "To get a hot dog and a beer at Fenway," he said, "it now takes a 36-month payment book."

The expansion New York Mets finished in last place their first three years, 1962–64, and, according to announcer Vin Scully, their supporters' expectations weren't much higher early in 1965. Scully reported that on Opening Day he saw a Mets fan with a sign that read, "Wait till next year!"

Red Sox announcer Ken Coleman was in Los Angeles doing the play-by-play for an Angels–Red Sox night game. In the late innings, aware that it was 2:00 A.M. back in Boston, he said, "That was a complicated play, so I'll go over it again for those of you scoring in bed."

Terry Felton pitched for the Twins for four years and did not win a game. He was, however, the hero of a typographical slip, thanks to Kansas City announcer Fred White. Noting that for a Twins game going on elsewhere, the scoreboard listed Felton both as the starting pitcher and as a second-inning relief pitcher, White said, "I see that in that Twins game, Terry Felton has relieved himself on the mound."

In the early eighties the Chicago White Sox defense was terrible. How bad was it? Announcer Jimmy Piersall pulled no punches: "They're missing

164

ground balls, fly balls, everything. I'm surprised they don't miss the dugout when they run in."

Young broadcaster Sherm Eagan was prepping for an interview he was about to do with Oakland's rich and famous owner, Charlie Finley. At one point, Finley said, "Don't call me Mr. Finley, Sherm; call me Charlie." "Gosh, thanks, Charlie," said Eagan. "Uh, not now, Sherm," said Finley. "Just during the interview."

In 1969 Yankees announcers Phil Rizzuto and Jerry Coleman agreed that the all-time Yankees outfield should include Mantle in left, DiMaggio in center, and either Maris or Charlie Keller in right. At this point an aide asked, "How about that fat guy for right field? Ya know, the one who boozed a lot and hit 60 home runs one year?"

Howard Cosell seems to have been equally disliked across all the sports he worked in. In baseball,

> When Howard Cosell lamented there being "so few great sports announcers today," a colleague quipped, "There's one fewer than you think, Howard."

Hall of Fame writer Red Smith said it for a lot of the scribes: "I have tried very hard to like Howard Cosell," he said, "and I have failed."

The L.A. Dodgers' Ron Cey was a National League All-Star for six straight years, was a consistent hitter, and drove in a lot of runs. But there were always questions about his mobility at third base. At one point, broadcaster Vin Scully said, "Pigeons have been roosting on him for two years."

To get some spontaneous reactions from Yogi Berra at a banquet, Ken Coleman, an announcer for the Red Sox, told him he was going to mention a number of players and wanted a one-word evaluation

from Yogi. Right off the top. One word. Got it, Yogi?
Yes. "OK," said Coleman. "First, Ted Williams." "What
about him?" said Berra.

George Steinbrenner
bought the Yankees in
1973, and it didn't take
baseball people long to
figure out that he intended
to be "the Boss." In 1981
announcer Jack Buck
resorted to a bit of
exaggeration to make the
point. Reporting on
George's new yacht, Buck
said, "It was a beautiful
thing to observe, with all
36 oars working in unison."

Dizzy Dean was as uninhibited as a broadcaster
as he was as a pitcher. During a Browns game, he
announced to the world, "Somethin's goin' on with

a fat lady down there behind the backstop." An embarrassed executive quickly took Dean aside to explain that the woman was a visiting royal dignitary. Dean recovered with, "Fans, ah've just been informed that the fat lady is the queen of Holland."

Howard Cosell was never at a loss for words. One anonymous admirer put it this way: "Cosell is a man who can talk for two hours on any given subject—four hours if he happens to know something about it."

It's no big news when a wild man like Babe Ruth or today's David Wells is out till the wee hours celebrating a big victory. But what about an introvert like the Dodgers' colorless, bland Burt Hooton? In 1978 Hooton won 19 games and led the Dodgers to the pennant, after which, according to announcer Vin Scully, "Burt went out and painted the town beige."

Chapter 14

THE COACHES, SCOUTS, AND MANAGERS, PART III

THE FACE THAT LAUNCHED A THOUSAND GIBES

Don Zimmer had three holes drilled in his head as a result of an early career beaning in 1953. His face has taken a few verbal hits, as well; his paunchy cheeks inspired the nickname "Gerbil," although not within his hearing.

Joe Garagiola contributed his own thoughts: "Don Zimmer's face looks like a blocked kick."

It always seemed that Zimmer was in training to become Casey Stengel. Returning from a road trip while managing the Cubs in 1990, Zimmer was unhappy with the club's 4–4 record.

"With a few breaks," he said, "it could have been just the other way around."

In 1984 Sparky Anderson took the Tigers all the way to a World Series title and was named American League Manager of the Year. The UPI's Milt Richman also nominated Sparky for the MVP . . . Most Voluble Person Award. "Sparky has a slight speech impediment," said Richman. "Every now and then he stops to take a breath."

Outfielder Cesar Cedano never played for manager Gene Mauch, but Mauch obviously admired his skills. When asked for his evaluation, Mauch said, "Cesar can play all three outfield positions . . . at the same time."

Part of Leo Durocher's success as a manager was his theory on scheduling starting pitchers: you simply start the best guy that's sitting there. "Never save a pitcher for tomorrow," he said. "It may rain tomorrow."

Gene Mauch was one of the better umpire baiters, and he knew how to harass an ump without getting tossed. Once, as his Montreal Expos charged out of the dugout to protest a call, Mauch, right behind them, yelled, "The first guy who lays a hand on that blind old man is fined 50 bucks!"

Casey Stengel knew how to deal with it when a TV reporter asked him, on camera, if his Yankees had choked when they lost the '57 World Series. "I said *f*—— to ruin his audio and scratched my ass to ruin his video," said Casey. "He ain't gonna ask me a question like that again."

Over 13 seasons, pitcher Geoff Zahn eked out a winning record despite having what some described as the slowest fastball in history. Manager Bob

Lemon said, "Some night Zahn is going to deliver the ball and by the time it gets there the batter will have been waived out of the league or traded."

Sharp-tongued manager Bill Rigney was put at a disadvantage as a bench-jockey when a car accident left him with his jaw wired shut. When asked if this limited his harassing of the umpires, Rigney said, "Not seriously. I can still hiss at 'em."

During the three years that Fred Haney managed the hapless St. Louis Browns (from 1939 to 1941), the team lost an average of 94 games each year. When management let him go, one of the local writers said that Haney wasn't fired—he was pardoned.

During his one year of managing the Oakland A's, Hank Bauer didn't get along too well with owner Charlie Finley. Once, sitting in his box, Finley phoned Bauer in the dugout and said, "When you went to the mound last inning I noticed grass stains on the back of your pants. That's a bad example." Bauer replied, "Those weren't grass stains, Charlie. That was mistletoe."

When Yogi Berra was managing the New York Mets, he was telling his old Yankees teammate Mickey Mantle about a couple of streakers at Shea Stadium. Mantle asked if they were men or women. "I don't know," said Yogi. "They had bags over their heads."

Ellis Clary knew he'd never get rich scouting for the Twins, so he always spent very frugally when working the bush leagues. A Twins front-office guy told of the time Clary had a heart attack while checking out a remote minor league game. As they were loading him into an ambulance, he said to the driver, "Get the mileage on this so I can put it on my expense report."

Pitcher Tug McGraw objected when manager Casey Stengel came out to pull him. "Come on, Casey," he said. "I can *get* this guy. I got him *last* time." "Yeah, I know," said Casey, "but the *last* time you got him was this same inning."

Brewers slugger Gorman Thomas knew how to release his anger. Yankees manager Bob Lemon recalled the time that Thomas fanned on a blooper pitch and was so mad that he tossed his batting helmet into the air and whacked it into short left field. "He missed the pitch," said Lemon, "but he sure got all of that helmet."

Chapter 15

THE HALL OF FAMERS, PART IV

A STACKED DECK

OK, so maybe this one isn't for real.

Maybe.

God decides to put together a baseball team, and on the first day of practice the devil calls to challenge God's team to a game. For serious money.

"You're crazy," says God. "I've got Ruth, Gehrig, Cobb, Cy Young—I've got all the players. Who have *you* got?"

"I've got all the umpires," says the devil.

* * *

At age 40, strong-willed Early Wynn made it clear that if and when he retired, it would be on his terms. "Somebody will have to come out to the mound and take the uniform off me," he said. "And the guy who comes out had better bring help."

No one ever doubted George Brett's will to win, but how did he feel about ties? Or even worse, losses? "If a tie is like kissing your sister," Brett once said, "a loss is like kissing your grandmother with her teeth out."

Grover Cleveland Alexander did not dawdle on the mound. Old Pete pitched so quickly that he practically invented the 90-minute ballgame—while winning 373 games. When criticized for his haste, he said, "What should I do, let them sons of bitches stand up there and think on my time?"

Reggie Jackson was, to put it mildly, something of a self-promoter. About the famous candy bar named after him, teammate Catfish Hunter said,

"When you unwrap one, it tells you how good it is." And writer Dave Anderson called it the only candy bar that tastes like a hot dog.

Hall of Famer Frankie Frisch batted .316 over his 19 years in the majors, but he averaged fewer than six home runs per year. One of them must have been a beauty, though. "Frisch's homer last week must have been the longest in history," said sportswriter Red Smith. "He talked about it all the way from St. Louis to Boston."

Leo "the Lip" Durocher was seldom at a loss for a comeback line. Coaching at third base during an exhibition game at West Point, he was zapped by a cadet in the stands. "Hey, Durocher," yelled the young man, "how did a little squirt like you make it to the majors?" "My congressman appointed me," said Leo.

During the 1970 World Series, Orioles third baseman Brooks Robinson dazzled fans and players alike with his spectacular fielding. After the final game, as reporters looked for Robinson, coach Rex Barney said, "He's not at his locker yet, but four guys are over there interviewing his glove."

When knuckleballer Joe Niekro was traded from the pinstriped Yankees to the pinstriped Twins in 1987, he was happy to escape all of New York's Steinbrenner-generated tension and dissension. "I'm still wearing pinstripes," he said, "but these don't have electrodes in them."

Cardinals pitcher Dizzy Dean was never the same after Cleveland center fielder Earl Averill hit him with a line drive in the 1936 All-Star Game.

And he had slipped even further when he was traded to the Chicago Cubs in 1938. "I ain't what I used to be," he said, "but who the hell is?"

The Yankees were up 1–0 in the bottom of the ninth of a typical Yankees–Red Sox game, in 1937. With two outs, Boston shortstop Joe Cronin stepped in. Johnny Broaca, pitching for the Yankees, *walked* Cronin to get at fearsome slugger Jimmy Foxx. Foxx crushed one that Joe DiMaggio saved with a miracle catch in deep center. "I was afraid of Cronin," said Broaca, "but I knew I could get Foxx."

The Brooklyn Dodgers had a number of ways to deal with Stan Musial. Preacher Roe said he'd walk Stan and try to pick him off first. Carl Erskine claimed that he had good luck just "throwing him my best pitch and backing up third."

189

Even while admitting that he consistently threw his greaseball to Rod Carew, Gaylord Perry still couldn't get the man out. "He must see the ball so well," said Perry, "that he can pick out the dry side."

Nolan Ryan holds two records that somewhat balance each other out. He leads all major league pitchers in lifetime strikeouts with 5,714, and his 2,795 walks lead the majors in that category. But his modesty prompted him to share the credit for the "most walks" mark. "I couldn't have done it without the umpires," he said.

Pitcher Lefty Gomez advised rookie Joe DiMaggio against playing such a shallow center field, the way the immortal Tris Speaker used to do it. DiMaggio replied that he was going to make people *forget* Tris Speaker. Slugger Hank Greenberg then drove a triple far over DiMaggio's head. Gomez said, "You keep playing there for Greenberg and you're going to make people forget Lefty Gomez."

In 2002, when the sometimes sullen Eddie Murray was inducted into the Hall of Fame, it prompted the *Chicago Sun-Times*' Rick Telander to point out that the Hall is not necessarily a Nice Guys' Club. "If you removed all the jerks from the Hall," he said, "it would be as crowded as the Ethics Room at Enron."

Chapter 16

THE PLAYERS, PART V

LIKE THE FOURTH OF JULY

Cubs pitcher Rick Sutcliffe was doing OK against the Reds in Cincinnati in a night game in 1989. But in the sixth inning the first batter hit one out, triggering a scoreboard fireworks display.

So did the second hitter. More fireworks.

As pitching coach Dick Pole strolled slowly to the mound, the irritated Sutcliffe yelled, "OK, let's go; are you pulling me or what?"

"No," said Pole, "the scoreboard guy just needs some time to reload."

*　*　*

In the early nineties Steve Lyons had an odd way of communicating with other American League second basemen. Like the time he drew an arrow out to the edge of the outfield grass and scrawled a note in the dirt: "Can you get to a ball way out here?" Next inning Lyons hit a ball to that exact spot and Seattle's Harold Reynolds threw him out. When Lyons returned to his position, Reynolds had written, "Yes."

In 1962 first baseman Marv Throneberry contributed to the Mets finishing 60½ games out of first by hitting .244 and leading the league in errors. Then, the following spring, he held out. The Mets' response was to ship Marvin off to their Buffalo farm club. Today this reaction is called "reality therapy."

When the *Denver Post*'s Jim Armstrong heard that longtime outfielder Jose Canseco had gotten a nose job to help him pursue an acting career, he had some advice. "I hope they don't cast him as an out-fielder," he said. "All those fly balls off the face were why he needed the nose job in the first place."

196

Pitching ace Greg Maddux
has never been known for
his speed on the base paths.
So when he actually legged
out a triple in a game
against the Marlins while he
was with Atlanta, an
engineer at Radio WSB said,
"It replaced the Kentucky
Derby as the most exciting
two minutes in sports."

After stints with both the Giants and the A's,
Bob Kearney finally became a regular catcher with
the Mariners in 1984. Even then he had to step
aside for Orlando Mercado whenever Salome
Barojas pitched. But Kearney understood. "I don't
speak Spanish," he said. *"C'est la vie."*

Is Pete Rose a quick study or what? In 1979,
after 17 seasons and, presumably, having heard the
"Star-Spangled Banner" sung at least 2,639 times, he

was heard to say, "Once the national anthem plays, I get chills. I even know the words to it now."

When Mitch Williams pitched for the Phillies he learned why the world's toughest sports fans are said to live in Philadelphia. After he blew a crucial save, a local restaurant posted a sign that read: "We reserve the right to refuse service to the following people: Mitch Williams."

Mention the name Bill Buckner and people immediately conjure up that fateful ground ball in Game 6 of the 1986 World Series against the Mets. But people forget that he hit only .188 in that Series. And they also forget what a less-than-great runner he was. How less-than-great? "The last guy who ran as badly as Bill Buckner," said sportswriter Mark Heisler, "was Long John Silver."

Who says they didn't have a smutty sense of humor back in the Roaring Twenties? St. Louis

Browns pitcher Al Sothoron didn't have a great year (8–15) in 1920, but during one game, his effort was commendable. Or, as one local newspaper put it, "Allen Sutton Sothoron pitched his initials off yesterday."

Sure White Sox slugger Frank Thomas can hit the long ball and drive in runs, but can he carry a team with his leadership qualities? The *Chicago Tribune*'s Rick Morrissey didn't think so. "Thomas could carry a bat made of beef jerky and not get a pack of wild schnauzers to follow him," he said.

During the 1984 World Series, the announcers were discussing the attributes that make a good-fielding first baseman. Joe Garagiola contended that

Dodger Gil Hodges had been so good because he had huge hands. "He wore a glove only because the other guys did," he said.

In ten years with the Angels and the Red Sox, second baseman Jerry Remy hit only seven home runs, and at one point there had been six years between dingers. After he ended that drought, Remy started to think hitting that homer hadn't been such a good idea. "Now the fans will expect me to hit one *every* six years," he said.

Dale Murphy caught a few games when he first came up with the Braves, and then went on to a long and successful career in the outfield. His father

had it all figured out early on. "My father said I would have been a great catcher if someone had tried to steal center field," said Murphy.

Darryl Strawberry found all kinds of ways to get into trouble, even in spring training where, with the Mets in 1989, he threw a punch at first baseman Keith Hernandez. *Sports Illustrated*'s Steve Wulf put his own spin on that one: "It was the only time Strawberry would hit the cutoff man all year."

Red Sox outfielder Jim Rice was big and strong, and he was never accused of having the best temperament in the league. When Roger Clemens was with Boston he was asked what kind of music they played on the team bus. "Whatever Jim Rice wants," he said.

Frank Sullivan pitched in the majors for 11 years, mostly for the Red Sox. He struggled for much of that time and didn't quite make it to a .500

career record. But he didn't have any illusions about his place in baseball history. Midway through his last season he said, "I'm in the twilight of a mediocre career."

In the mid-thirties, Babe Herman, the eccentric outfielder then with the Cubs, was complaining to a reporter about how the press depicted him as an oddball. At one point Babe pulled a cigar butt out of his pocket, put it in his mouth, and asked for a light. But before the newsman could produce a match, Babe said, "Never mind, it's lit."

Second baseman Emil Verban had almost 3,000 at-bats and clouted exactly one home run. He spent all or part of only three seasons with the Chicago Cubs, but he came to represent their long-standing pennantless frustrations. Writer George Will once called Verban the patron saint of Cubs fans because "he symbolizes mediocrity under pressure."

Pitcher Brian Anderson, the guy who once sleepwalked naked and locked his hotel door behind him, continues to prove that lefties are weird. In March 2003, scheduled to pitch an Indians exhibition game at the Dodgers' camp, he forgot to bring his glove and spikes and had to go out and buy some. Did he feel the need to improve his memory? "That's what spring training is for," he said.

Rocky Bridges just *may* have been confusing baseball with Asian food when, speaking of a game he once played against a Japanese team, he said, "An hour after the game you wanted to go out and play them again."

Do you think that first baseman J. T. Snow isn't conscious of his image *whatever* he's doing? In December of 2002 he had a chance to work one game as a water boy for the football Cardinals. When running back Marshall Faulk declined a drink during a timeout, Snow said, "C'mon, Marshall, *hydrate*. You gotta make me look *good* out here."

Jose Cruz Sr. was not the world's greatest fielder, but he certainly was not as bad as one teammate suggested. When Cruz caught the chicken pox early one season, the player said, "Maybe that's a good sign. Last year he didn't catch *anything*."

Orioles pitcher Mike Boddicker never did have a blazing fastball, so when, pitching at Toronto, he was clocked at 88 mph, teammate Mike Flanagan thought he had the answer. "We forgot to factor in the Canadian exchange rate," he said, "so it was really only 82 mph."

Late in a 1989 game against the Astros that went seven hours and 14 minutes, Dodgers third baseman Jeff Hamilton came in to throw to a couple of hitters and got off one pitch clocked at 91 mph. Since he hadn't pitched since high school, he attributed his high heat to a well-rested arm. He said he was pitching on seven years' rest.

Sammy Sosa's corked bat debacle in June of 2003 brought a lot of "cork" stories to the surface. Comedy writer Jerry Perisho, noting that, in theory, a corked bat allows a player to "move exterior girth at a faster speed," suggested, "The Mets might want to think about corking Mo Vaughn."

Chapter 17

THE HALL OF
FAMERS, PART V

REGULAR OR
DECAF?

Willie Stargell's sterling performance over 21 years got him into the Hall of Fame in 1988. Were there any pitchers he had trouble with?

"Hitting against Steve Carlton and Sandy Koufax," he said, "was like drinking coffee with a fork."

Koufax definitely knew where to put his blazing fastball.

He also knew how to deliver a stinging put-down. The last hit he surrendered, in his last game, was a single by Davey Johnson in the 1966 World Series. Years later, at a banquet, Johnson turned to Koufax and said, "Do you know I got the last hit you ever gave up?"

"I know," said Koufax. "That's why I retired."

Ask any of the hundreds of ex–major leaguers who ever faced Gaylord Perry if he threw the spitball and you'll get a unanimous affirmative. Ask Gaylord Perry and you'll get, "I may have thrown a few spitters, but just in the bullpen. I didn't want to be caught short in case they legalized it."

Pitcher Red Ruffing compiled most of his Hall of Fame stats while with the Yankees, but prior to that he spent seven years pitching for the Red Sox. Once, when called in from the bullpen to face the Yankees, he asked who was coming up. Upon being told it was Ruth, Gehrig, and Bob Meusel, he said, "Don't anybody touch that sandwich; I'll be right back."

Nineteen eighty was George Brett's big year. He flirted with the .400 mark all season and ended with a .390 batting average. He was especially tough against the Yankees, but pitcher Rudy May had a solution for the Brett menace. "You pitch him inside," he said. "That way he pulls it and the line drive won't hit you."

In 1964 Bob Gibson led the Cardinals to the N.L. pennant with 19 wins and then beat the Yankees twice in the World Series. When pitcher Roger Craig showed up for the team's 20th anniversary, he noted that the whole pitching staff was there except Gibson. "Of course," he said, "Bob Gibson *was* the whole pitching staff."

The great Mickey Mantle was larger than life, as were most of his home runs.

When cocky young Pee Wee Reese showed up in 1940 for his first training camp with the Dodgers, he approached Leo Durocher with, "So you're the guy I'm going to have to beat out for the shortstop job!" "Yeah," said Durocher. "And I'm still pretty good. I'm also still the manager."

Ty Cobb was not a pleasant competitor. The stories about him sharpening his spikes before a game are probably true. And pugnacious? Columnist Bugs Baer thought so. "Ty Cobb would climb a mountain to take a punch at an echo," he said.

Former fireballer Bob Feller showed a touch of humility a few years back when discussing some of his records. He pointed out that in addition to his strikeout numbers, he had given up eight bases-loaded home runs. What did that prove? "It showed that when I got into a jam I knew how to get out of it quickly," he said.

Apparently Mickey Mantle felt that first baseman Joe Pepitone thought too highly of his own talents. "I wish I could buy you for what you're *really* worth," said Mantle, "and sell you for what you *think* you're worth."

Perhaps Yogi Berra doesn't like to discuss unpleasant matters, or maybe he was just busy at the time, but when his wife asked him where he wanted to be buried, he said, "Surprise me."

Yankees pitcher Lefty Gomez had nightmares about Jimmy Foxx, the Red Sox's husky slugger, and his descriptions of Foxx were quite graphic. "He has muscles in his hair" was one explanation for Foxx's power. And how menacing was he at the plate? "He stands there with sawdust dripping off the end of the bat."

Chapter 18

AND OH YEAH, SOME OTHER GUYS, TOO

NOTHING BUT CHANGE-UPS

What do pro golfers do between PGA tournaments?

In late summer of 2003 Phil "Lefty" Mickelson decided to try out as a right-handed pitcher for Detroit's farm team, the Toledo Mudhens. He didn't get a contract, but he didn't embarrass himself, either.

Fellow golfer Paul Azinger had predicted success because "those hitters haven't seen a 68-mph fastball since Little League."

* * *

Football sportscaster Beano Cook is definitely not a baseball fan. When the American hostages in Iran were finally released in the early eighties, Commissioner Bowie Kuhn gave them all lifetime major league baseball passes. Beano's reaction: "Haven't they suffered enough?"

> Yankee Stadium may have its detractors, but all agree it's a magical place to play.

A *San Francisco Chronicle* reader claimed that when he recently umped a Little League game, one of the managers presented him with a lineup card that listed neither a pitcher nor a catcher. Why? "Batteries not included," he said.

American wrestler Rulon Gardner was huge when he won the superheavyweight title at the 2000 Olympics. He was also of "above average" size as a catcher in Little League baseball. "My strong suit was blocking the plate," he said. "I'd lie down and they couldn't find it."

Scott Ostler of the *San Francisco Chronicle* thinks that baseball is overly obsessed with statistics.

223

To illustrate, he says, "If you see an armored truck pull up outside a ballpark, it's not bringing cash; it's bringing boxes of decimal points."

> Everyone knows that spectator parents are the bane of Little League baseball, but what about all the stress and strain on the parents themselves? Columnist Earl Wilson said that, for the grown-ups, a Little League game is a "nervous breakdown divided into six innings."

Yankee Stadium is located in an area where you probably wouldn't want your mother window shopping late at night. Bill James, author of *The New Bill James Historical Baseball Abstract*, agrees: "If I were looking for Nazi Dr. Josef Mengele, my first thought would be to check the ushers at Yankee Stadium."

During the Yankees-Mets World Series of 2000, the city of New York tried hard to clean up its image. Jerry Greene of the *Orlando Sentinel*, while covering the games, claimed to have seen a sign that read: "As a gesture of good will, all wallets stolen on the subways will be returned for the duration of the Series."

Back when both Billy Graham and the Senators were headquartered in Washington, Graham was asked if prayer would help the hapless local team. "Prayer and about three outstanding pitchers," he replied.

The *Dallas Times*' Blackie Sherrod claimed that heckling must be permissible in baseball because eminent author George Bernard Shaw OK'd it for cricket. "There is no reason," Shaw insisted, "why the field should not try to put the batsman off his stride with neatly timed disparagement of his wife's fidelity and his mother's respectability."

In 1985 the Indians finished in last place in the American League East, 39½ games out. In September *L.A. Times* staffer and long-suffering Cleveland fan Dave Scheiderer said, "The Indians are so far behind they're already mathematically eliminated for *next* season."

The *Boston Globe*'s Ray Fitzgerald knew a guy who disliked the leisurely pace of baseball. He described it as "six minutes of action crammed into two and a half hours."

Baseball talent was probably never spread quite so thin as it was in 1945, when WWII was winding down. As the patchwork Cubs and Tigers limped into the World Series, questions arose about which team would take the fall classic. "I don't think either one can win it," said sportswriter Warren Brown.